CW00920161

The costs of
ACCIDENTS AT V

HSE BOOKS

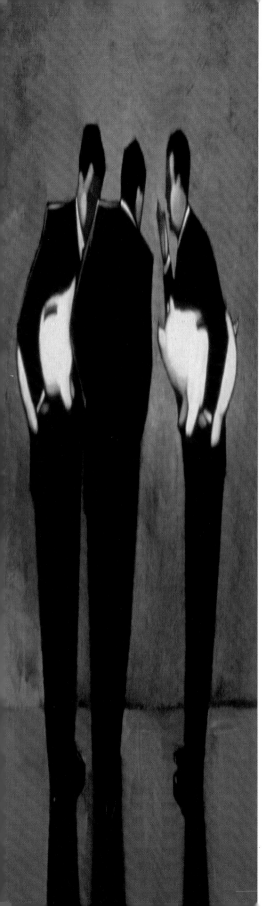

© Crown copyright 1997
Application for reproduction should be
made in writing to: Copyright Unit,
Her Majesty's Stationery Office,
St Clements House,
2-16 Colegate,
Norwich NR3 1BQ

First published 1993
Second edition 1997

ISBN 0 7176 1343 7

This guidance is issued by the
Health and Safety Executive.
Following the guidance is not
compulsory and you are free to
take other action. But if you do
follow the guidance you will
normally be doing enough to
comply with the law. Health and
safety inspectors seek to secure
compliance with the law and
may refer to this guidance as
illustrating good practice.

CONTENTS

FOREWORD

In 1993 HSE published the results of a series of case studies taken across a range of industries which demonstrated that few companies had any idea just what accidents at work really cost them, nor the means to find out. Since then the findings have been confirmed by further work in other industries and with smaller organisations.

My experience of talking to a wide range of businesses tells me that there is still a pressing need to emphasise the business case for good health and safety management. It is gratifying to note that these studies are now widely quoted both in other publications and at conferences which concern themselves with these issues.

In the Foreword to a *Financial Times* supplement published in November 1996 I made the point that many smaller organisations have little cushion against accidental losses and a serious accident could put them out of business. The supplement contains a number of new case studies where the scale of accidental losses has been recognised and cost-effective measures implemented.

At base, dealing with the causes of accidental losses is not an unnecessary overhead. Rather, failure to do so eats directly into the overall profitability of the company. HSE has no desire to impose needless burdens on anybody. On the contrary, taking to heart the lessons spelled out here can actually lighten the financial load.

Frank Davies

Frank J Davies CBE OStJ
Chairman, Health and Safety Commission

INTRODUCTION

Managers in industry know that accidents cost money. Whether people are injured, plant and machinery damaged or product wasted, organisations lose money.

Large scale losses such as those arising from major fires or explosions, or involving loss of life, are very visible and some have been costed on an individual basis. For example, the Piper Alpha explosion involved the loss of 167 lives and is estimated to have cost over £2 billion, including £746 million in direct insurance payouts. BP estimate that the refinery fire at Grangemouth in 1987, in which one person died, cost £50 million in property damage and a further £50 million due to business interruption.

Financial compensation for people who suffer injury at work is a considerable cost. According to the TUC, unions secured awards totalling £304 million for workplace injuries and ill health to their members in 1995. At an individual level there has been a recent award of £235 000 for back injuries suffered by a volunteer worker in a hospital. Less well understood, however, is the nature and extent of loss from accidents of a more routine nature: those accidents which injure but do not kill people, which damage plant and interrupt processes. The costs of these sorts of accident can often be hidden in sick pay, increased insurance premiums or maintenance budgets. Few firms have the mechanisms to identify them separately and fewer still actually identify and examine the costs of accidents systematically.

Twenty-five years ago the Confederation of British Industry (CBI), in evidence to the Robens Committee on Health and Safety at Work, said:

> "At the company level, if a readily applied and simple formula could be devised by which the financial loss caused by accidents and diseases could be measured..., it would make a valuable contribution towards reducing industrial accidents and occupational ill health."[1]

Since then, although there have been attempts to estimate the costs of accidents, usually concentrating on those involving personal injuries, there remains no generally accepted figure or methodology. Much of the previous work has focused on the retrospective analysis of data collected for other purposes such as litigation and insurance claims.

Against this background, in 1989 HSE's Accident Prevention Advisory Unit (APAU) - now Operations Unit (OU) - began a series of five case studies with organisations from various sectors of industry. The aim was to develop a methodology to accurately identify the full cost of accidents, to publish the results and thereby provide an incentive for all organisations to take the management of health and safety more seriously.

HSE has for many years advanced the view that there is no contradiction between health and safety and profitability; a view to which an increasing number of managers in industry subscribe. Those organisations which perform well and have high standards of health and safety are often the most successful, irrespective of size or industry. The common thread running through these organisations is the application of the principles of sound and effective management to health and safety, together with the integration of health and safety into their overall management agenda.

The Management of Health and Safety at Work Regulations 1992 now require employers to have effective arrangements in place for managing health and safety. HSE has published guidance on health and safety management. *Successful health and safety management*[2] is based on the principles of loss control and quality management. HSE's advice on these issues is not prescriptive and variations of approach may be necessary within individual organisations. However, an important common denominator is the adoption of a total loss control approach which seeks to identify and eliminate underlying failures of management control, irrespective of whether or not they lead to personal injury.

In loss control theory, the relationship between accidents is often expressed as accident pyramids. These pyramids are used to show the relationships between the numbers of accidents involving fatal injuries, non-fatal injuries, property damage and near misses, forming the peak, middle and base of the pyramids respectively.

The severity of the outcome of an accident often depends on chance if organisations fail to identify hazards and control risk. For example, if a person slips on a patch of oil leaked from a machine, the consequences may range from

soiled clothing to fatal injury. Coincidentally, the leaking oil may be a
contributory factor to machinery breakdown or lead to fire causing major or
minor damage. Therefore, as the precise outcome of an accident cannot be
predicted the only effective way to reduce accidents is to control the
underlying causes. Controlling the causes (inputs) of the patch of oil therefore
has the potential to prevent a whole range of possible consequences (outputs).

Managers now increasingly use the principles of loss control to minimise
accidental losses. In recent years the loss control approach has been
supplemented by the various schools of 'quality' management, including
aspirations to 'total quality'. [Total quality is defined as: 'a way of managing
to improve the effectiveness, flexibility and competitiveness of an organisation
as a whole'.[3]

The costings methodology developed by APAU attempted to identify the cost of all accidental losses that were considered to be preventable and that an organisation committed to loss control would aim to eliminate. To achieve this objective the methodology was based on a wide definition of the term 'accident'. **An accident was regarded as any unplanned event that resulted in injury or ill health of people, or damage or loss to property, plant, materials or the environment or a loss of business opportunity**. For a number of months in each of the five case studies, all accidents meeting this definition and involving loss above an agreed threshold were recorded. The cost of each accident was then assessed and a judgement made on whether it would have been cost effective to prevent it.

Detailed reports of the results from each study were agreed with the organisations concerned, together with publication of the main findings. The case studies are anonymised and information of a commercially sensitive nature has been omitted. The extent of financial savings which the organisations considered could be recovered by enhanced managerial control are identified.

The five studies produced results that could be compared with different operational parameters: for example, accidents cost:

■ one organisation as much as 37% of its annualised profits;

■ another the equivalent of 8.5% of tender price;

■ a third organisation 5% of its running costs.

None of the participating organisations suffered major or catastrophic loss during the study periods. Nor were there any fatal injuries, prosecutions or significant civil claims, all of which could have increased the levels of loss well beyond those recorded. A separate analysis of 80% of the accidents showed that over 8% were judged to have the potential for serious consequences such as fatalities, multiple injuries or catastrophic loss.

The significance of the findings, for the organisations concerned and industry in general, are likely to stimulate further debate and research. Measuring the costs of accidents is a complex matter and we are not yet in a position to produce the 'readily applied and simple formula' envisaged by the CBI, but our findings have built on the work of others and, we believe, provide well founded estimates of the costs of preventable accidental loss in the five organisations studied.

Organisations engaged in similar work activities to those studied, and indeed industry in general, should be able to relate to the results of the costings studies and draw comparisons. The methodology used to cost accidental loss in the five case studies is consistent with the treatment of the cost of non-conformance in quality costings. Accidental loss can therefore be readily integrated into quality cost findings.

Since the original publication further research has been undertaken with the aim of providing simplified costings methodologies more appropriate to smaller firms. This has resulted in the publication of a leaflet Be *safe, save money: the cost of accidents - a guide for small firms*.[4]

There is no legal requirement either to carry out costings studies or indeed record any information about the costs of an accident. HSE Operations Unit maintains an interest in such work, however, and is always pleased to advise organisations who wish to undertake such studies.

Summary of case studies' results and interpretation

The results of the five case studies show that it is possible to identify and quantify accurately the costs of preventable accidental loss arising from failures of management control. This has since been confirmed by further studies.

| The costs of accidental loss identified in each of the case studies were   *cost ceeline*
regarded by management as significant. Whether expressed as a percentage of operating costs (5%), tender price (8.5%) or extrapolated to annual losses (£3.76 million), in each case considerable sums of money were involved (Figure 1). |

Figure 1(a)   **Summary of losses identified***

		Total loss	Annualised loss	Representing
1	Construction site	£245 075	£700 000[†]	8.5% of tender price
2	Creamery	£243 834	£975 336	1.4% of operating costs
3	Transport company	£48 928	£195 712	1.8% of operating costs 37% of profits
4	Oil platform	£940 921	£3 763 684	14.2% of potential output
5	Hospital	£99 285	£397 140	5% of annual running costs

*   Figures quoted are actual at time of study: no adjustment has been made for inflation. Study 1 lasted 18 weeks; studies 2-5 13 weeks.

†   Represents total length of contract.

Figure 1(*b*)   **Average costs of an accident (£)**

	Accident type	Financial costs			Opportunity costs			Total costs		
		All	Injury	Non-injury	All	Injury	Non-injury	All	Injury	Non-injury
1	Construction site	24	0.4	26	43	8	46	71	8.4	72
2	Creamery	192	26	198	64	69	63	256	95	261
3	Transport company	37	-	37	111	-	111	148	-	148
4	Oil platform	2576	235	2657	361	469	357	2937	704	3014
5	Hospital	39	3	41	41	20	42	80	23	83
	Average all studies	157	21	161	64	54	63	221	75	224

In such a limited study it was not possible to establish how far the participating organisations were representative of their industries. However, it is reasonable to conclude that a similar picture, whether portrayed as total costs, numbers and types of accidents or insured/uninsured costs ratios, would emerge in other organisations with the final figures reflecting the extent and quality of their managerial control.

The costings methodology has been shown to work in a cross-section of industry and should prove workable in industry in general. Not all costings exercises need to be as resource intensive as the five developmental case studies; for example, sample studies could be undertaken within a department or production unit, and results interpreted for the organisation as a whole.

The case studies also demonstrate the differences between the insured and uninsured costs to the organisations concerned. These comparisons were made in four of the case studies where it was shown that uninsured costs were between 8 and 36 times greater than the costs of insurance premiums paid at the time of the studies (Figure 2). Many of the uninsured costs were in effect hidden, for example in maintenance and other budgets.

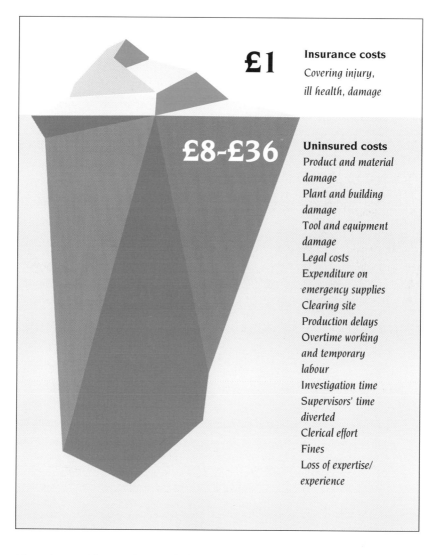

£1

Insurance costs
Covering injury,
ill health, damage

£8-£36

Uninsured costs
Product and material
damage
Plant and building
damage
Tool and equipment
damage
Legal costs
Expenditure on
emergency supplies
Clearing site
Production delays
Overtime working
and temporary
labour
Investigation time
Supervisors' time
diverted
Clerical effort
Fines
Loss of expertise/
experience

Figure 2   **Accident iceberg** - *the hidden cost of accidents*

The accident data which emerged from the case studies are summarised in Figure 3. The total number of accidents and figures for different types of accident are shown and accident pyramids based on these figures are also included. These pyramids illustrate the ratios between the accidents involving personal injury at varying levels of severity and non-injury accidents.

In each case there is a definable ratio between the numbers of property damage cases and personal injuries, although the exact ratios vary between the organisations studied. There are broad similarities between the pyramids for the creamery, oil platform and hospital. The base of the accident pyramid  is considerably wider in the construction study, with the number of reported accidents per staff year being over 10 times the average of the other four studies. At least part of this difference may be due to the changing nature of site conditions, compared with the routine of the more stable workplace environment. However, it is reasonable to assume that just as there are variations in the profiles of the pyramids for individual companies depending on the nature of their inherent risks and the level of management control applied, any pyramids developed to represent particular industries will also differ.

In all cases it was the management of the participating companies and/or steering group that identified the potential to prevent the accidents which were reported. They also acknowledged the value to them of identifying where accidental costs are incurred.

Figure 3   Five studies accident data

na   *not applicable*
*   *None recorded - about one expected from extrapolation from national construction accident data.*
†   *sign is used to indicate that value is a minimum ratio where no top event was recorded.*

Construction	Creamery	Transport	Oil platform	Hospital	All studies	All except construction	
18	13	13	13	13	70	52	Study period *weeks*
120	338	80	210	700	1448	1328	Number working on site
0	6	0	2	6	14	14	Over-3-day lost time injuries
56	31	0	8	58	153	97	Minor injuries
3570	889	296	252	1168	6175	2605	Non-injury accidents
3626	926	296	262	1232	6342	2716	Total accidents
1 / 56+ / 3570+	1 / 5 / 148	na	1 / 4 / 126	1 / 10 / 195	1 / 11 / 441	1 / 7 / 189	Accident ratios
1:64	1:24	na	1:25	1:18	1:37	1:23	Injury: Non-injury accident ratio
87	11	14	5	7	17	8	Accidents/ year/ employee
1:11	1:36	1:8	1:11	na	na	na	Insured to uninsured ratio costs

Main contractor only

13

Some of the commercial organisations have recognised that the investment needed to achieve an increase in market share to generate extra profits would be much greater than the investment needed to cut their accidental loss by a similar amount. They have therefore embarked on programmes to reduce accidents with the ultimate aim of minimising losses and eliminating personal injuries altogether. They have recognised the potential of management control strategies which selectively target the fundamental causes of accidents, starting at the base of their pyramid, to reduce the potential for major loss and personal injury.

These companies acknowledge that by incorporating health and safety management into wider campaigns associated with loss control and quality[20-22] they are not simply being altruistic; they are also reducing costs and improving the profitability of the business. This strategy is, of course, in addition to taking measures to deal with defects that are identified by risk assessments, inspections and investigations.

The HSE publication *Successful health and safety management*[2] gives guidance on developing effective health and safety management systems as part of an overall management control strategy. It suggests that a properly targeted programme of health and safety management applied in this way will reduce the human costs of ill health, injury and death, and the associated savings in financial costs will make for more efficient and profitable organisations. Furthermore, a properly targeted management programme aimed at accident prevention will ensure that health and safety objectives and legal obligations are met.

The costs of accidents at work describes findings in five organisations. In so far as they represent British industry, the national implications are striking. The results of the Labour Force Surveys for 1993/94, 1994/95, and 1995/96 indicate that each year about 1.1 million employed people in Great Britain sustained a workplace injury. In 1990 some 750 000 employees suffering from ill health caused or made worse by their work had to take time off.[10] This resulted in the loss of over 30 million working days and a cost to industry of almost £700 million. The overall cost of work accidents and work-related ill health to employers is estimated to be between £4000 million and £9000 million a year.[11]

This estimation includes the £750 million cost of paying employers' liability insurance to cover compensation to injured workers, the cost of recruiting and training replacements for those forced to give up work and the total cost of property loss. This is equal to between about 5% and 10% of gross trading profits. This does not include the costs that fall upon other sections of society, such as the cost of social security and NHS provision, and the financial and non-financial losses to the victims of accidents and occupational ill health. When these are taken into account, the total cost of work accidents and work-related ill health to society as a whole is estimated at between £10 billion and £15 billion a year - equivalent to between 1.75% and 2.75% of the country's gross domestic product.

CASE STUDIES

The case studies undertaken by HSE took place during 1990 and 1991. The sites chosen employed between 80 and 700 people and covered five different areas of employment. The participating organisations displayed average, or better than average, health and safety performance in their industries. It is likely that other organisations with less developed management systems would incur larger losses than those identified in these studies.

In each study, a steering group comprising staff from HSE and the participating organisation was established to direct the project. This group was the ultimate arbiter in cases of doubt. The studies identified the cost of accidents to the five organisations which in the opinion of the organisations' managers and the steering group could have been prevented. The studies were therefore 'owned' in equal measure by the organisations concerned and HSE. Detailed reports of each study were presented to and accepted by the organisations concerned.

Accident costs arising within each department were recorded using specifically designed forms. Subsequent forms were used by other departments to record their losses resulting from accidents elsewhere in the organisation. Further forms were completed on the costs of management time spent dealing with accidents.

It was not efficient to cost and record every minor loss and therefore a minimum reportable level of loss was agreed. Generally this was the minimum unit of product or its financial equivalent. Hence, a number of minor accidents were not recorded and the total numbers of accidents and associated costs in these studies may be regarded as slight underestimates. However, all identified personal injury accidents were included regardless of estimated loss. The number of accidents which resulted in major injury or caused absence in excess of three days, minor injuries and those which did not result in injury were all recorded in each of the case studies. The ratios between accidents of varying levels of severity were represented as accident pyramids.

Each recorded accident was examined by site management to decide whether it could have been prevented by the application of existing procedures or other cost-effective measures. Only those accidents judged to be economic to prevent were included. The methodology accounted separately for the financial and opportunity costs which arose from each accident.

Financial costs are the additional costs incurred to return the situation to what it was before an accident happened. This covers both material and labour costs.

Opportunity costs are the costs of lost opportunities, either through people having to stand idle or not being able to produce at their regular job by virtue of being redirected to deal with the consequences of an accident. This may not apply to the total cost of the company's overhead as some people such as firemen, nurses, cleaners and maintenance personnel are employed specifically for those tasks. There may be also energy costs from plant running idle and buildings being lit and heated.

Comparisons were also made between the ratio of insured and uninsured costs. This is represented as an iceberg showing the full costs of accidents, including those hidden below the water line. Organisations' insurance costs were taken to be the cost of insured premiums for the study periods. All types of insurance premium, such as employer's liability, were included. Many employers mistakenly believe they are covered by insurance for most of the costs arising from accidents. The study results show, however, that uninsured costs far exceed insured costs.

Previous work[5,6,7,8] has looked at the ratios of direct to indirect costs, but the precise meaning of this ratio has varied from author to author, making comparisons difficult. The advantage of analysing insured costs is that most organisations know how much and what types of insurance cover they have, and should be able to estimate their potential loss by comparison with a case study relating to a similar industry. In each case study the actual insurances held by the site are shown at the top of the iceberg. The amount and type of insurance cover held will vary. For example, if only third party vehicle insurance is held all own vehicle damage will be an uninsured cost.

CASE STUDY 1
CONSTRUCTION SITE

The longest of the studies, which took place over 18 weeks between June and November 1991, was carried out on the construction site for a supermarket. The main contractor was a wholly owned subsidiary of an international building and civil engineering company. Work on the contract, valued at about £8m, began in March 1991 and was completed in April 1992. Labour was provided primarily through 29 sub-contractors. A project manager was assigned to the site, along with two assistant site managers. Engineers were employed from an agency. The study took place over 18 weeks - the longest of all the studies. The duration and phasing (groundworks to roofing) were chosen to cover a range of stages of the construction process and, hence, a wide range of trade contractors.

Only £214 was lost when a five storey column fell over.

However, there was clearly potential for catastrophic loss

as a railway line was in reach of the column.

All accidents which met the accident definition, were above a threshold value of £5, and were considered by the main contractor to be preventable, were recorded for the whole site. A total of 3626 was recorded which resulted in direct financial losses of £87 507. Opportunity costs, mainly wages paid during periods of no production, amounted to a further £157 568, making a total loss of £245 075.

Assuming that accidents occurred at this rate throughout the entire contract, total losses were estimated to be in the order of £700 000, or approximately 8.5% of the £8m tender price. The costs of the recorded accidents to the main contractor alone were £79 709 (£21 106 financial and £58 603 opportunity costs).

Losses of this order are clearly important and particularly so in a recessionary climate, with tight margins for tenders in the construction industry. The financial costs alone represent significant lost potential for profit.

832 accidents were ascribed to inadequate planning and cost £41 680.

Fifty-six minor injuries and 3570 property damage accidents were recorded. It is to the company's credit that no major injuries, dangerous occurrences or over-3-day injury accidents occurred during the study period. National construction accident data[9] indicated that one over-3-day injury accident could have been expected during the study period. An accident pyramid was drawn (Figure 4) using the results from the study and the estimate from national accident data to give the appropriate accident ratios.

Over £2700 of damage and other losses resulted from 20 cases of vehicles and cranes hitting or running over property. Fortunately none of the accidents involved pedestrians.

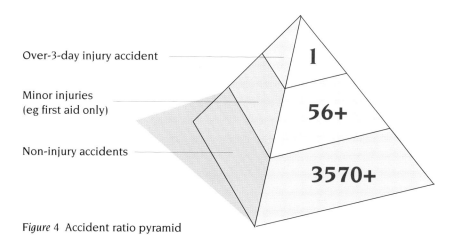

Over-3-day injury accident ⎯⎯⎯⎯⎯⎯ 1

Minor injuries
(eg first aid only) ⎯⎯⎯⎯⎯⎯ 56+

Non-injury accidents ⎯⎯⎯⎯⎯⎯ 3570+

Figure 4 Accident ratio pyramid

The accident pyramid (Figure 4) shows the largest ratio of non-injury accidents relative to injury accidents of any of the five studies. The construction industry generally has one of the highest reported injury incidence rates of all industrial sectors in the UK. If this study is representative of the industry it suggests that there is considerable scope for potential cost savings, by reducing accidental loss from accidents not involving person injury, which make up the base of the pyramid.

£124 was spent on cleaning the site following a leak

of sewage when part of a sewer diversion operation

went wrong. There was potential for pollution and ill

health, which fortunately did not occur.

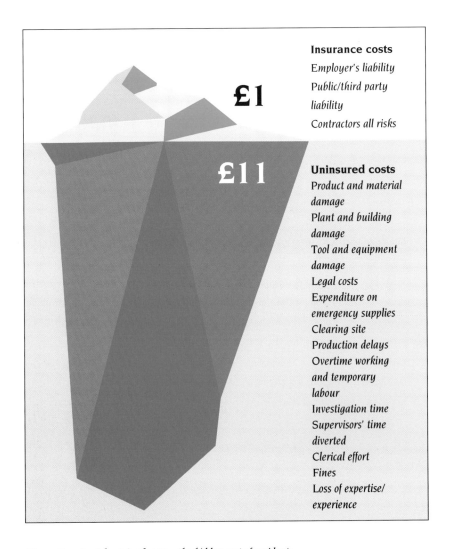

Insurance costs

Employer's liability

Public/third party liability

Contractors all risks

£1

£11

Uninsured costs

Product and material damage

Plant and building damage

Tool and equipment damage

Legal costs

Expenditure on emergency supplies

Clearing site

Production delays

Overtime working and temporary labour

Investigation time

Supervisors' time diverted

Clerical effort

Fines

Loss of expertise/experience

Figure 5 **Accident iceberg** - *the hidden cost of accidents*

The ratio of insured to uninsured costs incurred by the main contractor was 1:11 (Figure 5). The ratio for the whole site was not calculated as it was not possible to identify all the elements of insurance held by all the sub-contractors.

Some 1.6 million people work in the construction industry in Great Britain. Work on many medium and large sized sites is generally carried out by sub-contractors working for more major companies who manage the project. Even where accident costs are eventually met by sub-contractors, losses inevitably lead to a reduction in the efficiency of the site, which directly affects the management or main contractor. Such losses are important at any time, but with profit margins on tenders currently wafer-thin it is even more vital for the industry to keep costs to a minimum. The problems identified in this case study are likely to be common to all construction contracts and to any work won by competitive tender and involving extensive sub-contracting.

Lack of or poor supervision resulted in 594 accidents costing £26 384.

Nearly £500 of losses were incurred in six accidents when fork-lift trucks dropped their loads. There was potential for major injury or fatalities if any of the dropped loads had hit anyone.

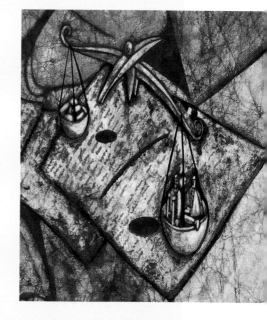

CASE STUDY 2
CREAMERY

A second study took place between March and June 1990 at one of a number of creameries owned by a leading UK manufacturer of dairy products. The manufacturer was in turn owned by a larger multi-national company. About 340 people worked at the creamery, organised into product and service departments. Each department had its own supervisors and manager under the direction of a general manager. There was a range of continuous and batch processes on site and night shifts operated in some departments.

During the study the creamery received up to 300 000 gallons of milk a day, collected from over 400 dairy farms, for processing into a range of dairy products. Other work activities included producing colourings, flavourings and packaging for products. Products were sold primarily to large supermarket chains, which imposed strict contractual requirements relating particularly to food quality and hygiene and the timeliness of deliveries. Most of the products had short shelf lives so there was a continual need to keep machinery and equipment in good working order to maintain production. The site was in the final stages of gaining certification to BS 5750 Part 2 *Quality systems*.

£2000 worth of damage was caused when a seal of the correct size but wrong specification was fitted to a machine following a breakdown. In other circumstances of non-adherence to specification, major accidents have resulted.

The study included periods of high and low demand for the company's products. A 'no-blame' policy was adopted for the duration to encourage staff to report all accidents. A total of 926 accidents were recorded, resulting in financial losses of £184 253. This was equivalent to 1.05% of operating costs during the study period. Opportunity costs, at £59 581, increased this figure to 1.4%. The total cost of all accidents recorded was £243 834. Accidents which cost less than £5 or 15 minutes lost time were not recorded.

Of the 926 accidents, six resulted in over-3-day injuries and a further 31 injuries required first-aid treatment. For each serious injury there were five minor injuries and 148 accidents involving damage to property and other non-injury losses. Ratios between these different types are represented in the accident pyramid (Figure 6).

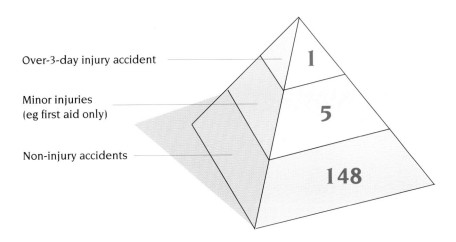

Over-3-day injury accident

Minor injuries
(eg first aid only)

Non-injury accidents

Figure 6   **Accident ratio pyramid**

The ratio of insured to uninsured costs was 1:36 (Figure 7). The difference between this ratio and that recorded in the other studies is partly accounted for by variations in insurance carried by different organisations. The important point is that in each study the figure for uninsured costs far outweighed insured costs.

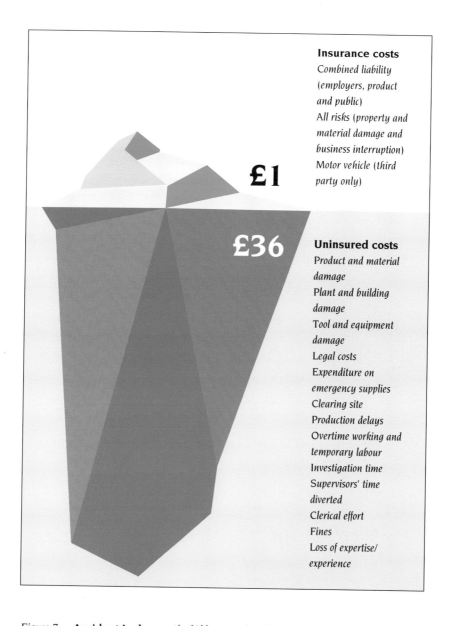

Insurance costs
Combined liability (employers, product and public)
All risks (property and material damage and business interruption)
Motor vehicle (third party only)

£1

£36

Uninsured costs
Product and material damage
Plant and building damage
Tool and equipment damage
Legal costs
Expenditure on emergency supplies
Clearing site
Production delays
Overtime working and temporary labour
Investigation time
Supervisors' time diverted
Clerical effort
Fines
Loss of expertise/ experience

Figure 7   **Accident iceberg** - *the hidden cost of accidents*

Over £3000 of losses resulted from three separate occasions of bacterial contamination of equipment used for handling the company's product. All the contaminations were identified and contained, but these accidents had the potential for major losses if public health had been affected.

A large number of accidents happened around the start of a shift at 6.00 am. However, the electricians and mechanics needed to carry out repairs were unavailable until 8.00 am because of the nature of the company's shift system. Following presentation of the study results to the company this problem was largely resolved by providing key machine operators with further training so that they could carry out some of the routine preventative maintenance tasks themselves. This subsequently considerably reduced the number of accidents and lost time experienced by the company.

£8200 of losses were caused when blocked bag filters became over-pressurised. Five tonnes of milk powder were lost in the exhaust air. While a dust explosion did not occur and no one was injured, the risk of a milk dust explosion had not been fully assessed.

£1800 of damage was caused when a road tanker was driven away while still connected to the factory pipework. Management had not identified the full potential of this hazard nor assessed the risk involved. If, for example, a flammable liquid had been involved rather than the company's comparatively innocuous product, there could have been a major accident involving the risk of fire and explosion.

The lessons from this particular study could be applied to some chemical companies as many of the processes undertaken at the factory were similar to those carried out in chemical production plants, although the nature of the materials handled will be different. However, the potential for major catastrophes did exist, for example the risk of fire or explosion during the handling of powdered milk and the possibility of microbiological contamination of both ingredients and products with the potential for a food poisoning outbreak.

Case study 3
Transport company

A third study took place at a transport company between March and June 1990. The company employed 80 people and was part of the same organisation which owned the creamery, although it was separately managed. The company operated a fleet of milk tankers on behalf of the Milk Marketing Board and collected milk from farms and delivered it to the creamery for processing. The company then delivered produce from the creamery to the regional distribution centres of major supermarkets throughout the UK. About 65 vehicles were based at the site and there was a maintenance department responsible for servicing both these and a further 80 refrigerated vehicles based elsewhere.

£2248 of damage was caused to vehicles manoeuvring at low speed in confined spaces. In many of these cases there was a risk of injury to nearby pedestrians but in the event no one was actually hurt.

A total of 296 accidents was recorded. Financial losses resulting from these accidents amounted to £16 215. Opportunity costs amounted to an extra £32 713. The total cost of the accidents recorded was £48 928 which represented 37% of annualised profits. Total accident costs represented 1.8% of operating costs.

£1150 was the cost when a drawbar was damaged,

there being no replacement available on site.

None of the accidents resulted in personal injury, therefore an accident pyramid could not be prepared. However, labour costs of vehicle repairs alone equated to one mechanic working two and a half days a week and in the week immediately following the study three major road traffic accidents occurred.

Uninsured losses were eight times higher than the insurance premiums paid during the period of the study (Figure 8).

The results of this study should be generally applicable to medium-sized transport companies with their own workshops.

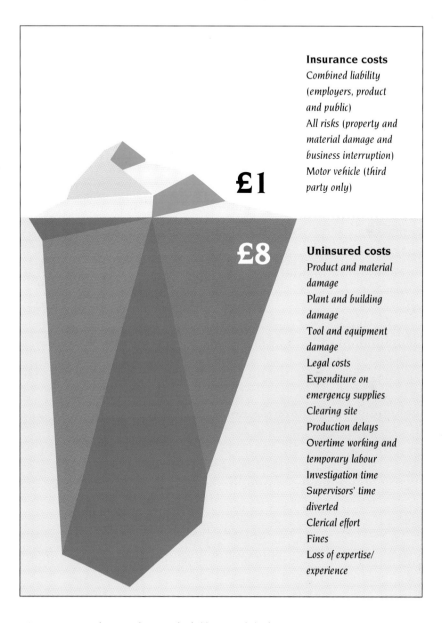

Insurance costs
Combined liability (employers, product and public)
All risks (property and material damage and business interruption)
Motor vehicle (third party only)

£1

£8

Uninsured costs
Product and material damage
Plant and building damage
Tool and equipment damage
Legal costs
Expenditure on emergency supplies
Clearing site
Production delays
Overtime working and temporary labour
Investigation time
Supervisors' time diverted
Clerical effort
Fines
Loss of expertise/ experience

Figure 8   **Accident iceberg** - *the hidden cost of accidents*

CASE STUDY 4
NORTH SEA OIL PRODUCTION PLATFORM

A fourth study took place between October 1990 and February 1991 at an oil production platform operated by an international oil company. The platform was one of a number that the company operated in the North Sea. The company was engaged in world-wide exploration, production and marketing of crude oil and natural gas. It manufactured and marketed finished products refined from crude oil. It also traded in and transported crude oil, liquefied natural gas, refined products and other commodities by tanker and pipeline.

The platform was situated in approximately 400 ft of water and was located 100 miles from land. It was staffed during the study by between 100 and 120 people including a number of sub-contractors. The plant and equipment operated continuously. Staff worked 12-hour shifts and were divided into two teams which alternated between the platform and shore leave.

> *An operative hit his hand with a 7 lb hammer - cost £2200. This high figure resulted from the high costs of obtaining treatment and underlines the variations in costs that can occur depending on circumstances of particular cases.*

The minimum recordable loss was set at half a barrel of oil (or its financial equivalent) or one hour of lost time. Two hundred and ninety-nine accidents were recorded, two of which involved absence from work for more than three days. A further eight needed first-aid treatment. Thirty-seven of the accidents, costing £24 822, were judged to be unpreventable. Excluding these 37, the 262 remaining produced an accident ratio of 1:4:126 for the platform (Figure 9), with financial costs of £847 079 and opportunity costs of £93 842, giving total accident costs of £940 921.

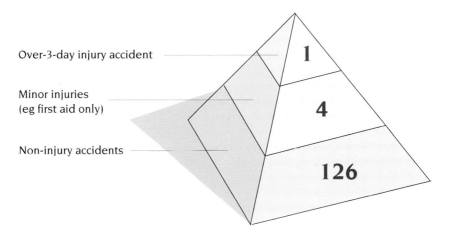

Over-3-day injury accident

Minor injuries
(eg first aid only)

Non-injury accidents

Figure 9   **Accident ratio pyramid**

The study was undertaken during a period when uninterrupted production was anticipated. There was little drilling activity, no planned shut-downs and no diving operations. The company considered that the accidents recorded and the production profiles during the study period were representative of a typical three-month operating window for the platform, based on the experiences of recent years. The total losses identified equated to a £3.76 million loss on an annual basis or to shutting down the platform for one day a week.

Many of the accidents recorded resulted either directly or indirectly in loss of oil production. The loss of oil was calculated on the value of the oil to the company and excluded the substantial tax element. The ratio between insured and uninsured costs was 1:11 (Figure 10), which was similar to the ratios from the other studies with the exception of the creamery.

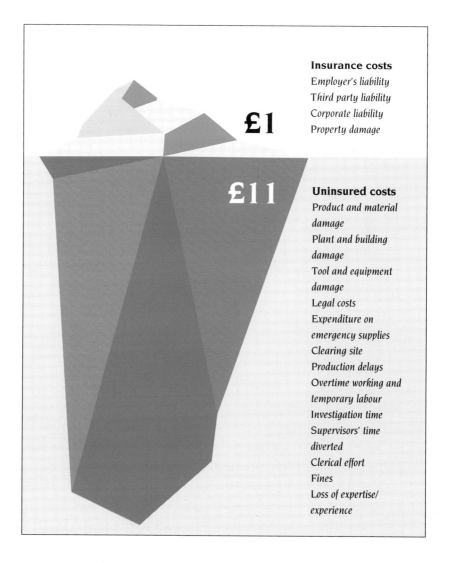

Insurance costs
Employer's liability
Third party liability
Corporate liability
Property damage

£1

£11

Uninsured costs
Product and material damage
Plant and building damage
Tool and equipment damage
Legal costs
Expenditure on emergency supplies
Clearing site
Production delays
Overtime working and temporary labour
Investigation time
Supervisors' time diverted
Clerical effort
Fines
Loss of expertise/ experience

Figure 10   **Accident iceberg** - *the hidden cost of accidents*

Just before the study started, a 'Downtime Advisory Team' had been set up to look into production loss. As a result of the HSE study the terms of reference of this team were broadened to address all preventable losses. The team were charged with the task of developing methods to measure and analyse losses occurring on the platform, and therefore made timely use of HSE's methodology.

£3496 was the cost when a control room operator cleared an 'inhibit' imposed as part of a permit-to-work system, without realising that the 'inhibit' was required for a second hot work permit. As a result 8 tonnes of fire foam were automatically released, the platform workers assembled at emergency muster stations, and the standby vessel steamed closer to the platform.

At the time of the study the company was in the process of introducing a loss control system. Subsequently the system was implemented on all platforms and warehouse facilities in a bid to develop health and safety management and improve loss control in general. Costing techniques developed from HSE's methodology were refined by the company and extended to other areas of operation. The results of this study should be applicable to oil and gas production platforms, onshore oil and gas installations, and other chemical processing sites.

In this particular study an accident potential matrix* was used to identify the potential for injury and loss that could have resulted from accidents, given slightly differing circumstances (Figure 11).

* The potential matrix used in this case study was developed by Shell UK Exploration Production, operators in the UK sector of the North Sea, on behalf of Shell, Esso and other co-venturers.

Figure 11 **North Sea oil production platform – accident potential analysis**

Actual

Injuries/damage	A	B	C	D	E
Minor injuries/miscellaneous damage, no business impact: eg cut, strain or damage to equipment	12	7			
Moderate injuries/damage with some business impact: eg fracture/burn/smoke emission/moderate damage	229	4			
Severe injuries/damage/business impact: eg loss of sight of eye, major fracture, minor fire	40				
Fatality, explosion with moderate damage, significant adverse business impact	7				
Multiple fatality, or explosion with major loss/ catastrophic business and/or environmental impact					
	0	1	2-10	11-100	100+

Number of persons affected/at risk

Worst credible outcome

Injuries/damage	A	B	C	D	E
Minor injuries/miscellaneous damage, no business impact: eg cut, strain or damage to equipment	10	8			
Moderate injuries/damage with some business impact: eg fracture/burn/smoke emission/moderate damage	88	4	1		1
Severe injuries/damage/business impact: eg loss of sight of eye, major fracture, minor fire	103	1			
Fatality, explosion with moderate damage, significant adverse business impact	79			3	1
Multiple fatality, or explosion with major loss/ catastrophic business and/or environmental impact					
	0	1	2-10	11-100	100+

Number of persons affected/at risk

The top matrix assigns the 299 accidents which occurred to a series of boxes dependent upon their actual outcome. Each accident was then analysed individually and assigned to a particular box on the bottom matrix dependent upon what *could* have happened on a worst credible case scenario basis. Five accidents were agreed with the company as having the potential for either fatality or moderate injury involving a large number of people.

Over £360 000 of total losses were recorded for 84 non-injury accidents which were judged to have the potential for significant adverse business impact, or loss of life.

As the case study lasted only 13 weeks it was statistically unlikely that major or catastrophic events would be recorded, and in the event none were. Use of the matrix allowed the company to identify those accidents with potential for more serious consequences and so target their preventative resources to best effect.

Case study 5
NHS HOSPITAL

The fifth study was carried out between March and June 1991 at a hospital which employed about 700 people and belonged to a large metropolitan Health Board. The hospital had 367 beds, seven care of the elderly wards, a plastic and oral surgery unit, and an annual budget of £8m. Following the Government's reforms of the National Health Sevice (NHS), the management structure of the hospital was in the process of being changed at the time of the study. The hospital was striving to deliver a higher quality service and to shorten waiting lists, as part of a general initiative within the NHS.

During the study 1232 accidents were recorded. This resulted in a direct financial cost to the hospital of more than £48 000. In addition there were opportunity costs of around £51 000, making a total of just under £100 000. On an annual basis this equated to around £397 000 or 5% of the hospital's annual running costs. These figures are thought to be conservative. Reluctance by some medical staff to participate fully in the study meant a number of accidents went unreported.

> *Costs of nearly £7000 resulted from a major oil spillage when a tanker driver failed to follow the correct filling procedure and so attempted to fill an already full oil storage tank. In addition to the losses actually incurred, this accident resulted in an increased fire hazard and had the potential for major injuries and environmental damage.*

Six injuries led to three or more days' absence, 25 accidents involved personal injuries to staff, 38 to patients and one to a visitor. For every accident resulting in a 3-day-injury, ten resulted in minor injuries and a further 195 resulted in non-injury accidents (Figure 12).

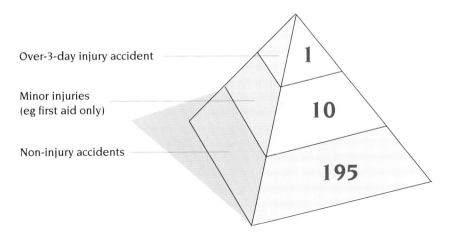

Over-3-day injury accident — 1

Minor injuries (eg first aid only) — 10

Non-injury accidents — 195

Figure 12   **Accident ratio pyramid**

Many losses were directly attributable to poor preventative maintenance of equipment, plant and hospital buildings. This affected the quality of service provided by the hospital, as well as staff and patient morale. It was not possible to put a money cost on the effect on patients as, unlike the other studies, loss, damaged or poor quality products could not be costed. The ratio of insured/uninsured costs could not be calculated in this case as the NHS is self-insured.

£550 was lost when a transformer overheated due to inadequate maintenance, and smoke affected three floors of one hospital unit. Operating theatres were put on evacuation standby while the rest of the unit was evacuated. The relatively low cost in this case was due to the fact that some consequences, eg inconvenience to patients, could not be costed. Had the operating theatres been evacuated while in use, the financial and other consequences would have been more serious.

FURTHER INFORMATION ON LOSS CONTROL AND HEALTH AND SAFETY MANAGEMENT

For more than 20 years, some industrialists and leading health and safety professionals have argued that high health and safety standards are not only ethically desirable but, if pursued as part of a wider strategy of management control, can help reduce an organisation's costs. This argument has not secured universal acceptance because its validity in actuarial terms has not been conclusively demonstrated, as the exact extent of preventable loss has not been identified.

Managers have tended to focus on identifiable costs, namely those involved in complying with health and safety legislation: they have regarded these costs as a drain on their budgets. While some organisations have made significant advances in their health and safety performance, others have failed to perceive the economic advantage of improving standards.

Several authors have explored the links between the costs of accidents and the management of health and safety.[12-18] Others have argued that the key principles of quality management, in particular quality costing and the design of quality control and assurance systems, have direct relevance to modern health and safety management programmes.[19-22] Fisher,[22] for example, has classified the costs associated with quality and safety functions into prevention, appraisal and failure costs and has explored the links between the management of quality and health and safety. He argued that even for relatively unsophisticated organisations, failure costs can be greater than the combined prevention and appraisal costs.

One costing model is presented in Figure 13. This combines the prevention and appraisal costs as the total costs of the control programme. The second component represents the costs of the programme failure. Figure 13 shows that at some point further investment in the control programme will not give a net return (point A). However few, if any, leading companies consider that they have reached this point: many believe that they need to invest further in the managerial control of accidental loss.

The 'costs of the control programme', for example, include:

- decision making;
- safety hardware, eg ventilation systems, guards;
- communication and training time;
- publicity campaigns;
- ongoing inspection and auditing effort;
- maintenance;
- programme co-ordinator and support staff costs.

The 'costs of programme failures', for example, include:

- major and minor personal injury accidents;
- occupational ill health;
- equipment and material damage events;
- product losses;
- process and technical breakdowns or damage to the environment.

These programme failure losses arise primarily from failures of management control, and if not prevented or contained, can interact and escalate into larger losses.

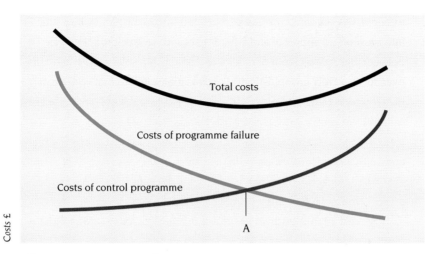

Costs £

Effort put into management control programme

Figure 13 **Economics of management control**

There are also intangible costs due to programme failures, for example loss of business image, customer satisfaction, employee morale, goodwill and reduced productivity. These intangibles were considered in the five studies described earlier, but could not be quantified in financial terms.

The graph in Figure 13 is essentially the same as for quality costings and those familiar with BS 6143 *Guide to the economics of quality*[23] may find it helpful to think of the following equivalencies:

■ 'costs of control programme' = cost of conformance;

■ 'costs of programme failures' = cost of non-conformance; and

■ 'total costs' = process costs.

The outcome of any particular accident is often a matter of chance: factors combine and take effect so that a near miss, minor injury or serious injury may all result from similar sets of circumstances. If the circumstances that lead to minor accidents can be controlled, those same controls will also prevent other accidents with more serious consequences, resulting from the same management failings.

Since the early 1970s APAU/OU has examined and analysed the management of health and safety and accident prevention in a large number of organisations. On the basis of this work it has concluded that a comprehensive system of accident prevention is necessary to achieve success in occupational health and safety management. Focusing on the prevention of reported personal injury accidents is not enough. There need to be proactive management control programmes which prevent or control **all** potential sources of loss.

In 1989 APAU, assisted by HSE's statisticians and economic advisers, began to develop and apply a methodology to measure the costs to organisations of failing to control accidental loss. The work, carried out by HSE staff alongside site management and financial specialists, built upon existing knowledge about accidents costings and the assumptions implicit in the accident pyramids produced by Heinrich,[5] Bird[6,23] and Tye.[24]

Heinrich argued that in order to eliminate injuries to people managers must tackle the root causes of accidents that lead randomly to injury. Total loss control theory uses the pyramid concept to show that controlling the numerous non-injury accidents will reduce the chance of injuries and fatalities, and so provide proactive control of health and safety.

The case studies described in this publication have extended the work of Heinrich[5] and others[6,7,12-16] and quantified the cost of personal injuries, property damage and other consequential losses to the five participating organisations. Third party costs, for example the costs of NHS treatment, the loss of business incurred by a customer when a supplier failed to deliver on time or the costs to those individuals injured, were not included. The significance of the case studies is that, for the first time, the costs of all individual accidents during the study periods were recorded as they occurred. The results are therefore actual costs - not estimates.

Fundamental to the loss control approach underlying the case studies is the view that by applying control systems which eliminate the underlying causes of accidents at the base of the pyramid, accidents in the rest of the pyramid will also be reduced (Figure 14). This view is based on the belief that although there is a wide range of **immediate causes** of accidents in the pyramid, the **underlying causes** are common. The majority of accidents have the potential to result in both property damage and personal injury. This is not, however, true in all cases: some injury accidents are unlikely to be associated with property damage, and some accidents which cause property damage have no potential to cause injury.[25]

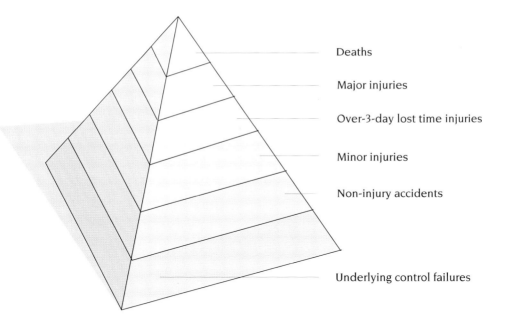

Deaths

Major injuries

Over-3-day lost time injuries

Minor injuries

Non-injury accidents

Underlying control failures

Figure 14 **The accident pyramid**

It must not be forgotten that there are circumstances where health and safety legislation requires action to prevent personal injury, irrespective of the level of loss that may be associated with it. Increasingly these circumstances are defined by risk assessment which identifies the hazards and associated risks and helps target prevention and control.

References

1   *Safety and Health at Work* Robens Committee Report Vol 2 (Cmnd 5034)
     HMSO 1972 ISBN 0 10 150340 7

2   *Successful health and safety management* HS(G)65 HSE Books 1993
     ISBN 0 7176 0425 X

3   Oakland, Professor John S, *Total Quality Management: a practical approach*
     (2nd edition) February 1994 Butterworth Heinman ISBN 0750 609 931

4   *Be safe, save money: the costs of accidents - a guide for small firms* IND(G)208L
     HSE Books Single copies free, multiple copies available in priced packs
     ISBN 0 7176 1018 7

5   Heinrich H W, *Industrial accident prevention* (4th edition)
     New York McGraw-Hill 1959

6   Bird F E and Loftus R G, *Loss control management* Loganville,
     Georgia, Institute Publishing 1976 ISBN 0 88061 0000 X

7   Leopold E and Leonard S, Costs of construction accidents to employers
     Journal of Occupational Accidents 1987 8 273-294

8   *From drawing board to building* Publication EF/81/17/FR HMSO London
     ISBN 0 11 701576 8

9   Health and Safety Commission *Annual Report* 1991/92 HMSO 1992
     ISBN 0 11 882073 7

10   *The 1990/91 Labour Force Survey* OPCS HMSO 1992 ISBN 0 11691387 8

11   Davies MV and Teasdale P, *The costs to the British economy of work accidents
     and work-related ill health* HSE Books 1994 ISBN 0 7176 0666 X

12   Veltri A, An accident cost impact model: the direct cost component
      Journal of Safety Research 1990 21 67-73

13   Brody B, Letourneau Y and Poirier A, An indirect cost theory of work
      accident prevention *Journal of Occupational Accidents* 1990 13 255-270

14   Wright E L G, True costs of accidents are not assessed *Australian Safety*
      News December 1990 61 (11)

15   Andreoni D, *The Cost of Occupational Accidents and Disease* Occupational
      Safety and Health Series 54 International Labour Office Geneva 1986
      ISBN 92 2 103758 4

16   Soderqvist A, Rundrno T and Aaltonen M, Cost of occupational accidents
      in the Nordic furniture industry (Sweden, Norway, Finland)
      Journal of Occupational Accidents 1990 12 (1-3) 79-88

17   Sachs B, Accidents - an avoidable waste *Safety Management*
      February 1991 17(2) 23

18   Brody B, Letourneau Y and Poirier A, The cost of industry accidents
      Current State of Knowledge 1991

19   Salazar N, Applying the Deming Philosophy to the safety systems
      Professional Safety December 1989 34(12) 22-27

20   Whiston J and Eddershaw B, Quality and safety - distant cousins or close
      relatives? *The Chemical Engineer* June 1989 No 461 97-102

21   Pardy W G, Do the right thing. The safety/quality relationship
      Canadian Occupational Safety September/October 1991 29(5) 10-12,14

22   Fisher T, A 'quality' approach to occupational health, safety and rehabilitation *Journal of Occupational Health and Safety - Australia and New Zealand* 1991 7(1) 23-28

23   BS 6143 *Guide to the Economics of Quality* Part 1 Process Cost Model 1992

23   Bird F E and Germain G L, *Practical Loss Control Leadership* Loganville, Georgia, Institute Publishing 1985 ISBN 0 88061 054 9

24   Tye J, *Accident Ratio Studies* 1974-1975 British Safety Council 1976

25   Parkes M J, *The Accident Triangle - A Valid Tool?* In the Health and Safety Practitioner, October 1993

Printed and published by the Health and Safety Executive   5/97   C70